Kahlil Gibran's

LITTLE BOOK OF LOVE

Kahlil Gibran's

LITTLE BOOK OF LOVE

Neil Douglas-Klotz

HAMPTON ROADS

Cover design by Jim Warner
Cover photograph Crazy in Love by Rebecca Campbell/Private
    Collection/Bridgeman Images
Interior by Deborah Dutton
Typeset in ITC Garamond Std

Hampton Roads Publishing Company, Inc.
Charlottesville, VA 22906
Distributed by Red Wheel/Weiser, LLC
www.redwheelweiser.com

Sign up for our newsletter and special offers by going to
www.redwheelweiser.com.

ISBN: 978-1-57174-833-1
Library of Congress Cataloging-in-Publication Data

Names: Gibran, Kahlil, 1883-1931 author. | Douglas-Klotz, Neil
    editor author of introduction.
Title: Kahlil Gibran's little book of love / Neil Douglas-Klotz
    [editor].
Other titles: Little book of love
Description: Charlottesville, VA : Hampton Roads Publishing
    Company, 2018. | In English with some selections originally
    translated from Arabic.
Identifiers: LCCN 2018018565 | ISBN 9781571748331 (5 x 7 pbk.
    w/ flaps : alk. paper)
Classification: LCC PS3513.I25 A6 2018 | DDC 818/.5209--dc23
LC record available at https://lccn.loc.gov/2018018565

Printed in Canada
MAR

10   9   8   7   6   5   4   3   2   1

FOR ALL THE LOVERS SEPARATED BY
ANOTHER'S ILLUSION OF THE OTHER

Contents

2. The Veils of Love 45

3. All Our Relationships 91

4. A Love Beyond 133

Sources of the Selections 181

Introduction

Kahlil's Gibran's aphorisms, stories and poetry on the theme of love remain some of those best known to Western readers. The Lebanese-American writer's views, however, extend beyond the most-quoted, "greeting card" sayings to a very wide realm of human relationships—passion, desire, idealized love, justice, friendship, and the challenges of dealing with strangers, neighbors and enemies.

These new "little book" collections take a fresh look at Gibran's words and wisdom, taking into account the major influences in his life: his Middle Eastern culture, nature mysticism and spirituality. One could easily argue that what the average reader of Gibran in the 1920s found exotic was the way he clearly expressed a region that most regarded as a conundrum. Nearly a hundred years later, understanding the Middle Eastern conundrum—especially regarding human relationships and the treatment of the "other"—has moved from the level of a philosophical problem to become a practical matter of everyday survival.

The book before you collects Gibran's words on love and relationships. The first in the series collected his writings on life and nature. The next book will focus on life's paradoxes and the mysteries of the inner path, and the final one on wisdom for daily life, both in solitude and in community.

At first glance, Gibran may seem to be a romantic, a poet of idealized love. Yet he was not a sentimentalist. He understood from his own experience the darker side of relationships—longing, sorrow, loss, lust and passion—and its value in helping the soul's journey through life. Rather than espousing a Platonic love "beyond the flesh," neither soul nor body gets preferential treatment in his writings.

One sees several influences here. First, Gibran's personal love relationships were fraught throughout his short life. As his various biographers relate, no personal testimony, especially his own, can be taken at face value as "what happened" (see "About the Author" at the back of this book). Even in Gibran's recounting of his first love in "The Broken Wings," we find long dialogues or monologues that stretch credibility in terms of what we might call factual reporting. In his defence, we could say that Gibran was aware that different people can have very different recollections of important incidents or conversations, especially those concerned with love. Such events make an emotional impact on memory that influence us in ways we can often only explain to ourselves much later, or not at all.

Second, Gibran's Middle Eastern language and culture offer very nuanced views of love, which reveal the small emotional corner into which we have painted ourselves through the over-sexualized content found today on the internet, in popular films and in advertising.

Like many languages, Gibran's native Arabic has several different words that can be literally translated as "love."

One concerns love's desire and passion (the word *ishq*), which we could describe as the magnetism that draws individuals together (like the force of gravity) and attaches them to each other like glue. This "glue of the universe" operates above, below and beyond our logical, human intentions. The phrase "I couldn't help myself" is apropos here. The Song of Songs in the Jewish scriptures describes this force of burning passion between two lovers exquisitely in Hebrew. At the same time, some early Sufi poets identify this relentless force of love and passion with God or Reality itself.

Another ancient Semitic word for love (*ahaba* in Hebrew, *ahebw* in Jesus' Aramaic, *muhabbah* in Arabic) concerns the varieties of human relationship, which emerge as a seed of respect or tolerance, then sprout into friendship and blossom as intimate, enduring love. Another image presented by the languages' roots show a small flame sparked from kindling, which gradually becomes a large fire, good for cooking and warming oneself.

Yet another word for love (*rahm* in Hebrew, *rahme* in Aramaic, *rahman* and *rahim* in Arabic) derives from that for *womb*. The word's roots imply that physical birth originates as a radiance that comes from inside. This same creative radiance develops into what we call compassion, mercy or unconditional love.

The word for "heart" is similarly very old in the culture. The Hebrew *leba* and the Aramaic *lebha* both show a creative force that is the essence or center of one's life. The Arabic words *lubb* and *qalb* derive from these earlier ones, the latter word revealing that that the heart can have a changing surface as well as a stable depth. While today we highly prize the brain as the essential organ of consciousness, the ancients in the Middle East valued the heart much more. Perhaps this is why the ancient Egyptians preserved the physical hearts of their royalty after mummification and tossed the brain away. They felt the pharoahs would need the heart in the afterlife, the brain not so much.

As I noted in the previous collection on "life," Sufi poetry and storytelling was a major influence on Gibran. Take for instance, one of his sayings on love, from the book *Sand and Foam*:

Love is the veil between lover and lover.

Then compare it to one from the 13th century Sufi poet Jelaluddin Rumi:

The Beloved is all in all, the lover only a veil over her.

The idea of love revealing and veiling, of a veritable house of mirrors that influences our relationships, was spoken about in the Sufi poetry from early on, yet only recently articulated in the Western psychological language of projection and transference. Again from Gibran:

Lovers embrace that
which is between them
rather than each other.

At the same time, Gibran beautifully expresses the Middle Eastern view that love, whether expressed in pleasure or pain, in a passionate embrace or in intense unfulfilled longing, can lead one to a much larger sense of life. This collection draws on Gibran's incredible late book on Jesus entitled *Jesus The Son of Man*. In a very modern way, Gibran tells the prophet's story from the viewpoints of many different people who knew him, some mentioned in the Bible, others not. In this little book on love, we hear several times from Mary Magdalene, from Salome (who danced for King Herod then demanded John the Baptist's head) from a neighbor of Jesus' mother, from Judas' mother and from the apostles Peter and John.

As I noted in the earlier collection, Gibran was raised as a Maronite Christian, an Eastern church allied to the Roman Catholic, but that until the 18th century, spoke and used in liturgy the Syriac language, related to Jesus' native Aramaic. The Aramaic-speaking churches historically viewed Jesus, the prophet of Nazareth as a human being, a small-s "son" of God, who uniquely fulfilled his destiny and expressed the divine life in a way open to all of us. In this sense, we can all become "children" of God, that is, of "Sacred Unity" (the literal translation of the Aramaic word for God, *Alaha*).

Consistent with this, toward the end of *Jesus The Son of Man*, Gibran has Mary Magdelene say:

> There is a gulf that yawns between those who love him and those who hate him, between those who believe and those who do not believe.
>
> But when the years have bridged that gulf you shall know that he who lived in us is deathless, that he was the son of God even as we are the children of God. That he was born of a virgin even as we are born of the husbandless earth.

Yet in writing of love, Gibran breaks through the boundaries of conventional religion in any form. In one of his most daring works, a poetic cycle entitled "The Earth Gods," Gibran has the ancient gods of earth bemoan the predictability of life and its boring routine. They have almost talked themselves into full-fledged funk when one of them notices a lover and beloved singing and dancing, then embracing and making love in the middle of the forest. This changes everything, and the old gods are simultaneously baffled and thrilled by the unpredictable power of love's passion. I have included the "love" parts of this work, but the whole poem is worth the reader's attention.

In all of his writings, Gibran's love for his native land and people shines through. When he left Lebanon with his family in 1895, it was still part of the Ottoman empire. Gibran saw himself as "Syrian" culturally (neither the states of Syria nor Lebanon existed before World War I), and throughout his life worked for the liberation of his people from oppressive regimes. He was disappointed by the way they were betrayed when Western powers carved up the Middle East into various countries and spheres of influence after the War. He took this betrayal personally, as a betrayal of friendship. In his essay "A Poet's Voice" from the book *A Tear and a Smile,* he laments:

> You are my brothers and sisters, but why are you quarrelling with me? Why do you invade my country and try to subjugate me for the sake of pleasing those who are seeking glory and authority?

I have included a number of selections from this essay and invite the reader to listen to Gibran's voice with the current conflicted situations in the Middle East in mind.

On the actual editing: it is clear that Gibran was helped with his grammar and punctuation by various people, particularly his long-time muse and editor Mary Haskell. As the way we read has changed over the past hundred years, so has grammar, so I have re-edited or re-lined many selections in order to bring out the rhythm of Gibran's voice for the modern reader.

As far as Gibran's use of gender-inclusive or exclusive terms go, I have mostly taken a hands-off approach. Throughout his writing, Gibran often refers to God as "he," but he also refers to Life as "she," and makes frequent references to "goddesses." In the total picture, things balance out, which is what one finds in reading gendered languages like ancient Hebrew or classical Arabic, where the sun, moon, and various living beings of nature have gendered forms. A good example in this collection is "The Love Song of the Wave," in which the sea (here feminine) embraces the shore (masculine). Instead of adhering to stereotypical human ideas of gender, Gibran asks us to expand beyond the human.

In one exception to this editing policy, I have substituted "humanity" for "mankind." This does not disturb the rhythm of Gibran's voice, is more faithful to the underlying (and gender neutral) Arabic word he was thinking of, and is a more accurate way of including us all. Likewise, I have made gender neutral one of the sections of Gibran's "poet's voice" pieces included here. Given current events in the Middle East, not so unlike what occurred in Gibran's time, I believe that this small change emphasizes the immediacy of his voice.

In selecting the material for this book, I have placed well-known sayings of Gibran next to lesser known ones, organized by the various faces and stages of love that his writing describes. We begin with love's initiation—beauty, passion and desire. After this comes love's many complexities and challenges, its veils. Then we explore the varieties of human relationship in which love plays hide-and-seek with us. Finally, we are led further on love's path, which points beyond our human lifespan.

As Rumi urges:

Whether you love God or love a human
     being,
if you love enough you will come into the
     presence of Love itself.

And as Gibran says wistfully toward the end of *The Prophet*:

A little while,
and my longing shall gather
dust and foam
for another body.

A little while,
a moment of rest
upon the wind,
and another woman shall bear me.

—Neil Douglas-Klotz
Fife, Scotland
October 2017

1

Love's Initiation

The spring of love introduces us to
beauty, desire and passion. What part
does the "smoke" of love play in relation
to love's enduring fire?

THE SPRING OF LOVE

Come, my beloved,
let us walk amidst the knolls.
For the snow is water,
and life is alive from its slumber
and is roaming the hills and valleys.

Let us follow the footprints of spring
into the distant fields,
and mount the hilltops to draw inspiration
high above the cool, green plains.

Dawn of spring has unfolded her
winter-kept garment and placed it
on the peach and citrus trees.
And they appear as brides in the
ceremonial custom of the Night of Kedre[1].

---

1. Also called Layat-ul Qadr, the "night of power." In the Islamic
   traditions, this is the night on which Prophet Muhammad first
   began to receive the Qur'an. It is marked on one of the last five
   days of the month of Ramadan. The night is said to hold spe-
   cial blessings and so was sometimes considered an auspicious
   time for a wedding in Lebanon.

The sprigs of grapevine
embrace each other like sweethearts,
and the brooks burst out in
dance between the rocks,
repeating the song of joy.
The flowers bud suddenly
from the heart of nature,
like foam from the rich heart of the sea.

Come, my beloved,
let us drink the last of winter's tears
from the cupped lilies
and soothe our spirits
with the shower of notes from the birds,
wandering in exhilaration
through the intoxicating breeze.

Let us sit by that rock where violets hide.
Let us pursue their exchange
of the sweetness of kisses.

BEAUTY IN THE HEART

There are only two elements here,
beauty and truth—
beauty in the hearts of lovers
and truth in the arms of
the tillers of the soil.

Great beauty captures me,
but a beauty still greater frees me,
even from itself.

Beauty shines brighter
in the heart of the one who longs for it
than in the eyes of the one who sees it.

First Love

I was eighteen years of age when love opened my eyes with its magic rays and touched my spirit for the first time with its fiery fingers. And Selma Karamy was the first woman who awakened my spirit with her beauty and led me into the garden of high affection, where days pass like dreams and nights like weddings.

Selma Karamy was the one who taught me to worship beauty by the example of her own beauty and revealed to me the secret of love by her affection. She was the one who first sang to me the poetry of real life.

Every young man remembers his first love and tries to recapture that strange hour, the memory of which changes his deepest feeling and makes him so happy in spite of all the bitterness of its mystery.

In every young man's life there is a "Selma," who appears to him suddenly while in the spring of life and transforms his solitude into happy moments and fills the silence of his nights with music.

I was deeply engrossed in thought and contemplation and seeking to understand the meaning of nature and the revelation of books and scriptures when I heard LOVE whispered into my ears through Selma's lips. My life was a coma, empty like that of Adam's in Paradise, when I saw Selma standing before me like a column of light. She was the Eve of my heart, who filled it with secrets and wonders and made me understand the meaning of life.

The first Eve led Adam out of Paradise by her own will, while Selma made me enter willingly into the paradise of pure love and virtue by her sweetness and love. But what happened to the first man also happened to me, and the fiery word that chased Adam out of Paradise was like the one that frightened me by its glittering edge and forced me away from the paradise of my love without having disobeyed any order or tasted the fruit of the forbidden tree.

Today, after many years have passed, I have nothing left out of that beautiful dream except painful memories flapping like invisible wings around me, filling the depths of my heart with sorrow and bringing tears to my eyes.

And my beloved, beautiful Selma is dead. And nothing is left to commemorate her except my broken heart and a tomb surrounded by cypress trees. That tomb and this heart are all that is left to bear witness of Selma.

The silence that guards the tomb does not reveal God's secret lying in the obscurity of the coffin. And the rustling of the branches, whose roots suck the body's elements, do not tell the mysteries of the grave. But the agonized sighs of my heart announce to the living the drama that love, beauty, and death have performed.

O friends of my youth who are scattered in the city of Beirut! When you pass by the cemetery near the pine forest, enter it silently and walk slowly so the tramping of your feet will not disturb the slumber of the dead. Stop humbly by Selma's tomb and greet the earth that encloses her corpse and mention my name with a deep sigh and say to yourself, "Here all the hopes of Gibran, who is living as a prisoner of love beyond the seas, were buried. On this spot he lost his happiness, drained his tears, and forgot his smile."

"By that tomb grows Gibran's sorrow together with the cypress trees. And above the tomb his spirit flickers every night commemorating Selma, joining the branches of the trees in sorrowful wailing, mourning and lamenting the going of Selma, who yesterday was a beautiful tune on the lips of life and today is a silent secret in the bosom of the earth."

O comrades of my youth! I appeal to you in the names of those virgins whom your hearts have loved to lay a wreath of flowers on the forsaken tomb of my beloved.

For the flowers you lay on Selma's tomb are like falling drops of dew from the eyes of dawn on the leaves of a withering rose.

WANDERING DESIRE

When you were a wandering desire in the mist,
I too was there, a wandering desire.

Then we sought one another
and out of our eagerness
dreams were born.

And dreams were time limitless,
and dreams were space without measure.

And when you were a silent word
upon life's quivering lips,
I too was there, another silent word.

Then life uttered us and
we came down through the years,
throbbing with memories of yesterday
and with longing for tomorrow.

For yesterday was death conquered
and tomorrow was birth pursued.

Singing the Heart

Our mind is a sponge.
Our heart is a stream.

When Life does not find
a singer to sing her heart,
she produces a philosopher
to speak her mind.

Beauty and Love

Beauty has its own heavenly language, loftier than the voices of tongues and lips. It is a timeless language, common to all humanity, a calm lake that attracts the singing rivulets to its depths and makes them silent.

Only our spirits can understand beauty, or live and grow with it. It puzzles our minds. We are unable to describe it in words. It is a sensation that our eyes cannot see, derived from both the one who observes and the one who is looked upon.

Real beauty is a ray that emanates from the holy of holies of the spirit and illuminates the body, as life comes from the depths of the earth and gives color and scent to a flower.

Did my spirit and Selma's reach out to each other that day when we met, and did that yearning make me see her as the most beautiful woman under the sun? Or was I intoxicated with the wine of youth, which made me fancy that which never existed?

Did my youth blind my natural eyes and make me imagine the brightness of her eyes, the sweetness of her mouth, and the grace of her figure? Or was it that her brightness, sweetness, and grace opened my eyes and showed me the happiness and sorrow of love?

It is hard to answer these questions. But I say truly that in that hour I felt an emotion that I had never felt before, a new affection resting calmly in my heart, like the spirit hovering over the waters at the creation of the world. And from that affection was born my happiness and my sorrow.

Thus ended the hour of my first meeting with Selma. And thus the will of heaven freed me from the bondage of youth and solitude and let me walk in the procession of love.

IF YOU HAVE DESIRES . . .

Love has no other desire but to fulfill itself.

But if you love and must have desires,
let these be your desires:

To melt and be like a running brook
that sings its melody to the night.

To know the pain of too much tenderness.

To be wounded by your own understanding
    of love
and to bleed willingly and joyfully.

To wake at dawn with a winged heart
and to give thanks for another day of loving.

To rest at the noon hour and meditate love's
     ecstasy.

To return home at eventide with gratitude
and then to sleep with a prayer
for the beloved in your heart
and a song of praise upon your lips.

DESCRIBING FIRST LOVE

A woman whom providence has provided with beauty of spirit and body is a truth, at the same time both open and secret. We can understand that truth only by love and touch it only by virtue. And when we attempt to describe such a woman, she disappears like vapor.

Selma Karamy had bodily and spiritual beauty, but how can I describe her to one who never knew her?

Can a dead man remember the singing of a nightingale, the fragrance of a rose and the sigh of a brook?

Can a prisoner who is heavily loaded with shackles follow the breeze of the dawn?

Is not silence more painful than death?

Does pride prevent me from describing Selma in plain words, since I cannot draw her truthfully with luminous colors?

A hungry man in a desert will not refuse to eat dry bread even if heaven does not shower him with manna and quails.

MISTAKEN IDENTITY

Upon a day Beauty and Ugliness met on the shore of a sea. And they said to one another, "Let us bathe in the sea."

Then they disrobed and swam in the waters. And after awhile Ugliness came back to the shore and clothed himself with the garments of Beauty and walked away.

And Beauty too came out of the sea and found not her raiment. And she was too shy to be naked, so she dressed herself with the raiment of Ugliness. And Beauty walked her way.

And to this very day men and women mistake the one for the other.

Yet there are some who have beheld the face of Beauty, and they know her, notwithstanding her garments. And there are some who know the face of Ugliness, and the cloth conceals him not from their eyes.

LOVE'S SUMMER

Let us go into the fields, my beloved.
For the time of harvest approaches,
and the sun's eyes are ripening the grain.

Let us tend the fruit of the earth,
as the spirit nourishes
the grains of joy
from the seeds of love
sowed deep in our hearts.

Let us fill our bins
with the products of nature,
as life fills so abundantly
the domain of our hearts
with her endless bounty.

Let us make the flowers our bed
and the sky our blanket
and rest our heads together
upon pillows of soft hay.

Let us relax after the day's toil
and listen to the provoking murmur
of the brook.

O LOVE

They say the jackal and the mole
drink from the same stream
where the lion comes to drink.

And they say the eagle and the vulture
dig their beaks into the same carcass
and are at peace, one with the other,
in the presence of the dead thing.

O Love, whose lordly hand
has bridled my desires,
and raised my hunger and my thirst
to dignity and pride,
let not the strong and constant in me
eat the bread or drink the wine
that tempt my weaker self.

Let me rather starve,
and let my heart parch with thirst.
And let me die and perish
before I stretch my hand
to a cup you did not fill
or a bowl you did not bless.

DESIRE IS HALF

Desire is half of life.
Indifference is half of death.

Between Desire and Peace

They say to me, "You must choose between the pleasures of this world and the peace of the next world."

And I say to them, "I have chosen both the delights of this world and the peace of the next. For I know in my heart that the Supreme Poet wrote but one poem, and it scans perfectly, and it also rhymes perfectly."

Faith is an oasis in the heart
that will never be reached by
the caravan of thinking.

When you reach your height,
you shall desire only for desire.
And you shall hunger only for hunger.
And you shall thirst only for greater thirst.

GOD MOVES IN PASSION

Your reason and your passion are the rudder and the sails of your seafaring soul.

If either your sails or your rudder be broken, you can but toss and drift, or else be held at a standstill in mid-seas.

For reason ruling alone is a force confining. And passion unattended is a flame that burns to its own destruction.

Therefore let your soul exalt your reason to the height of passion that it may sing.

And let it direct your passion with reason, that your passion may live through its own daily resurrection, and like the phoenix rise above its own ashes.

I would have you consider your judgment and your appetite even as you would two loved guests in your house.

Surely you would not honor one guest above the other. For the one who is more mindful of one loses the love and the faith of both.

Among the hills, when you sit in the cool shade of the white poplars, sharing the peace and serenity of distant fields and meadows, then let your heart say in silence, "God rests in reason."

And when the storm comes, and the mighty wind shakes the forest, and thunder and lightning proclaim the majesty of the sky, then let your heart say in awe, "God moves in passion."

And since you are a breath in God's sphere, and a leaf in God's forest, you too should rest in reason and move in passion.

VOICES IN RAPTURE

[The ancient Earth Gods, weary and depressed,
converse among themselves about life's purpose,
or the lack of it, until one of them notices....]

A youth in yonder vale
is singing his heart to the night.
His lyre is gold and ebony.
His voice is silver and gold.

Down in the myrtle grove
a girl is dancing to the moon,
a thousand dew-stars are in her hair,
about her feet a thousand wings.

The girl has found the singer!
She sees his raptured face.
Panther-like she slips with subtle steps
through rustling vine and fern.

And now amid his ardent cries
he gazes full on her.

O my brothers, my heedless brothers!
Is it some other god in passion
who has woven this web of scarlet and white?
What unbridled star has gone astray?
Whose secret keeps night from morning
and whose hand is upon our world?

They meet,
two star-bound spirits
in the sky encountering.

In silence they gaze
one upon the other.
He sings no more,
and yet his sunburnt throat
throbs with the song.
And in her limbs
the happy dance is stayed
but not asleep.

Brothers, my strange brothers!
The night waxes deep,
and brighter is the moon,
and between the meadow and the sea
a voice in rapture calls you and me.

YOUR BODY IS THE HARP
OF YOUR SOUL

But tell me, who is the one that can offend the spirit?

Shall the nightingale offend the stillness of the night, or the firefly the stars?

And shall your flame or your smoke burden the wind?

Do you think the spirit is a still pool that you can trouble with a staff?

Oftentimes, in denying yourself pleasure, you only store the desire in the recesses of your being.

Who knows whether that which seems omitted today waits for tomorrow?

Even your body knows its heritage and its rightful need and will not be deceived.

And your body is the harp of your soul.

It is yours to bring forth sweet music from it or confused sounds.

And now you ask in your heart, "How shall we distinguish that which is good in pleasure from that which is not good?"

Go to your fields and your gardens, and you shall learn that it is the pleasure of the bee to gather honey of the flower.

But it is also the pleasure of the flower to yield its honey to the bee.

For to the bee a flower is a fountain of life, and to the flower a bee is a messenger of love.

And to both bee and flower, the giving and the receiving of pleasure is a need and an ecstasy.

If Your Heart Is a Volcano

If your heart is a volcano
how shall you expect flowers
to bloom in your hands?

I am the flame
and I am the dry bush.
And one part of me
consumes the other part.

Love Across Age

The poet youth said to the princess, "I love you."

And the princess answered, "And I love you too, my child."

"But I am not your child. I am a man and I love you."

And she said, "I am the mother of sons and daughters, and they are fathers and mothers of sons and daughters. And one of the sons of my sons is older than you."

And the poet youth said, "But I love you."

It was not long after that the princess died. But before her last breath was received again by the greater breath of earth, she said within her soul,

"My beloved, mine only son, my youth-poet, it may yet be that someday we shall meet again, and I shall not be seventy."

A DESIRE UNFULFILLED

Salome speaks about Jesus to a woman friend:

He was like poplars
shimmering in the sun.
And like a lake among the lonely hills,
shining in the sun.
And like snow upon the mountain heights—
white, white in the sun.

Yea, he was like all these,
and I loved him.

Yet I feared his presence,
and my feet would not carry
my burden of love
that I might girdle his feet
with my arms.

I would have said to him,
"I have slain your friend in an hour of passion.
Will you forgive me my sin?
And will you not in mercy release my youth
from its blind deed
that it may walk in your light?"

I know he would have
forgiven my dancing
for the saintly head of his friend.
I know he would have seen in me
an object of his own teaching.

For there was no valley of hunger
he could not bridge,
and no desert of thirst
he could not cross.

Yes, he was even as the poplars
and as the lakes among the hills
and like snow upon Lebanon.

And I would have cooled my lips
in the folds of his garment.

But he was far from me,
and I was ashamed.
And my mother held me back
when the desire to seek him was upon me.

Whenever he passed by,
my heart ached for his loveliness,
but my mother frowned at him in contempt
and would hasten me from the window
to my bedchamber.

And she would cry aloud saying,
"Who is he but another locust-eater from the
    desert?
What is he but a scoffer and a renegade,
a seditious riot-monger,
who would rob us of sceptre and crown,
and bid the foxes and the jackals of his
    accursed land to
howl in our halls and sit upon our throne?
Go hide your face from this day,
And await the day when his head shall fall
    down,
but not upon your platter."

These things my mother said.
But my heart would not keep her words.

I loved him in secret,
and my sleep was
girdled with flames.

He is gone now.
And something
that was in me
is gone also.

Perhaps it was my youth
that would not tarry here,
since the god of youth was slain.

A Passion Unspent

In the city of Shawakis lived a prince, and he was loved by everyone—men, women and children. Even the animals of the field came to him in greeting.

But all the people said that his wife the princess loved him not. Nay, that she even hated him.

And one day the princess of a neighboring city came to visit the princess of Shawakis. And they sat and talked together, and their words led to their husbands.

And the princess of Sharakis said with passion, "I envy you your happiness with the prince, your husband, though you have been married these many years. I hate my husband. He belongs not to me alone, and I am indeed a woman most unhappy."

Then the visiting princess gazed at her and said, "My friend, the truth is that you love your husband. Aye, and you still have him for a passion unspent. And that is life in a woman, like spring in a garden. But pity me and my husband, for we only endure one another in silent patience. And yet you and others deem this happiness."

ALL THE STARS OF MY
NIGHT FADED AWAY

Mary Magdalene speaks about meeting Jesus for the first time:

It was in the month of June when I saw him for the first time. He was walking in the wheat field when I passed by with my handmaidens, and he was alone.

The rhythm of his steps was different from other men's, and the movement of his body was like nothing I had seen before.

Men do not pace the earth in that manner. And even now I do not know whether he walked fast or slow.

My handmaidens pointed their fingers at him and spoke in shy whispers to one another. And I stayed my steps for a moment and raised my hand to hail him. But he did not turn his face, and he did not look at me. And I hated him. I was swept back into myself, and I was as cold as if I had been in a snowdrift. And I shivered.

That night I beheld him in my dreaming. And they told me afterward that I screamed in my sleep and was restless upon my bed.

It was in the month of August that I saw him again through my window. He was sitting in the shadow of the cypress tree across my garden, and he was as still as if he had been carved out of stone, like the statues in Antioch and other cities of the North Country.

And my slave, the Egyptian, came to me and said, "That man is here again. He is sitting there across your garden."

And I gazed at him, and my soul quivered within me, for he was beautiful. His body was single, and each part seemed to love every other part.

Then I clothed myself with raiment of Damascus, and I left my house and walked towards him.

Was it my aloneness or was it his fragrance that drew me to him? Was it a hunger in my eyes that desired comeliness, or was it his beauty that sought the light of my eyes?

Even now I do not know.

I walked to him with my scented garments and my golden sandals, the sandals the Roman captain had given me, even these sandals.

And when I reached him I said, "Good-morrow to you."

And he said, "Good-morrow to you, Miriam."

And he looked at me, and his night-eyes saw me as no man had seen me. And suddenly I was as if naked, and I was shy.

Yet he had only said, "Good-morrow to you."

And then I said to him, "Will you not come to my house?"

And he said, "Am I not already in your house?"

I did not know what he meant then, but I know now.

And I said, "Will you not have wine and bread with me?"

And he said, "Yes, Miriam, but not now."

Not now, not now, he said. And the voice of the sea was in those two words, and the voice of the wind and the trees. And when he said them to me, life spoke to death.

For mind you, my friend, I was dead. I was a woman who had divorced her soul. I was living apart from this self that you now see. I belonged to all men and to none. They called me harlot, and a woman possessed of seven devils. I was cursed, and I was envied.

But when his dawn-eyes looked into my eyes, all the stars of my night faded away, and I became Miriam, only Miriam, a woman lost to the earth she had known, and finding herself in new places.

And now again I said to him, "Come into my house and share bread and wine with me."

And he said, "Why do you bid me be your guest?"

And I said, "I beg you to come into my house."

And it was all that was sod in me, and all that was sky in me, calling unto him.

Then he looked at me, and the noontide of his eyes was upon me, and he said, "You have many lovers, and yet I alone love you. Other men love themselves in your nearness. I love you in your self. Other men see a beauty in you that shall fade away sooner than their own years. But I see in you a beauty that shall not fade away. And in the autumn of your days that beauty shall not be afraid to gaze at itself in the mirror, and it shall not be offended. I alone love the unseen in you."

Then he said in a low voice, "Go away now. If this cypress tree is yours and you would not have me sit in its shadow, I will walk my way."

And I cried to him and I said, "Master, come to my house! I have incense to burn for you, and a silver basin for your feet. You are a stranger and yet not a stranger. I entreat you, come to my house!"

Then he stood up and looked at me, even as the seasons might look down upon the field, and he smiled. And he said again, "All men love you for themselves. I love you for yourself."

And then he walked away.

But no other man ever walked the way he walked. Was it a breath born in my garden that moved to the east? Or was it a storm that would shake all things to their foundations?

I knew not, but on that day the sunset of his eyes slew the dragon in me, and I became a woman. I became Miriam, Miriam of Mijdel.

2

The Veils of Love

As love matures, we are challenged by
our surrounding culture as well as by
the unspoken assumptions and illusions
we hold. Tears come with parting, lone-
liness and longing. Through all these
experiences, love veils and unveils itself.

LOVE'S GIFTS

Love provided me with
a tongue and tears.

THE CAGED HEART

There in the middle of the field, by the side of a crystalline stream, I saw a bird cage whose rods and hinges were fashioned by an expert's hands. In one corner lay a dead bird and in another were two basins—one empty of water and the other of seeds.

I stood there reverently, as if the lifeless bird and the murmur of the water were worthy of deep silence and respect—something worthy of examination and meditation by the heart and conscience.

As I engrossed myself in view and thought, I found that the poor creature had died of thirst beside a stream of water and of hunger in the midst of a rich field, a cradle of life. It was like a rich man locked inside his iron safe, perishing from hunger amid heaps of gold.

Before my eyes I saw the cage turn suddenly into a human skeleton and the dead bird into a human heart, which was bleeding from a deep wound that looked like the lips of a sorrowing woman.

A voice came from that wound saying, "I am the human heart, prisoner of substance and the victim of earthly laws.

"In God's field of beauty, at the edge of the stream of life, I was imprisoned in the cage of laws made by humanity.

"In the center of beautiful creation I died neglected, because I was kept from enjoying the freedom of God's bounty.

"Everything of beauty that awakens my love and desire is a disgrace, according to human conceptions. Everything of goodness that I crave is but naught, according to this judgment.

"I am the lost human heart, imprisoned in the foul dungeon of human dictates, tied with chains of earthly authority, dead and forgotten by laughing humanity, whose tongue is tied and whose eyes are empty of visible tears."

All these words I heard, and I saw them emerging with a stream of ever-thinning blood from that wounded heart.

More was said, but my misted eyes and crying soul prevented further sight or hearing.

Love v. Law

Those people who go to back to eternity before they taste the sweetness of real life are unable to understand the meaning of a woman's suffering.

Especially when she devotes her soul to a man she loves by the will of God, and her body to another whom she caresses by the enforcement of earthly law.

THREE PERSONS SEPARATED

Three persons were separated in thought but united in love, three innocent people with much feeling but little knowledge.

A drama was being performed by: an old man who loved his daughter and cared for her happiness, a young woman of twenty looking into the future with anxiety, and a young man, dreaming and worrying, who had tasted neither the wine of life nor its vinegar, and was trying to reach the height of love and knowledge but was unable to lift himself up.

We three, sitting in twilight, were eating and drinking in that solitary home, guarded by heaven's eyes, but at the bottoms of our glasses were hidden bitterness and anguish.

What Lovers Embrace

Lovers embrace that
which is between them
rather than each other.

Two Kinds of Love

A man and a woman sat by a window that opened upon spring. They sat close to one other.

And the woman said, "I love you. You are handsome, and you are rich, and you are always well-attired."

And the man said, "I love you. You are a beautiful thought, a thing too apart to hold in the hand, and a song in my dreaming."

But the woman turned from him in anger, and she said, "Sir, please leave me now. I am not a thought, and I am not a thing that passes in your dreams. I am a woman. I would have you desire me, a wife and the mother of unborn children."

And they parted.

And the man was saying in his heart, "Behold, another dream is even now turned into mist."

And the woman was saying, "Well, what of a man who turns me into a mist and a dream?"

Whom Do We Love?

When I stood, a clear mirror before you,
you gazed into me and saw your image.

Then you said, "I love you."
But in truth you loved yourself in me.

Love is the veil between lover and lover.

LAUGHTER AND TEARS

As the sun withdrew its rays from the garden, and the moon threw cushioned beams upon the flowers, I sat under the trees, pondering upon the phenomena of the atmosphere, looking through the branches at the strewn stars, which glittered like chips of silver upon a blue carpet. And I could hear from a distance the agitated murmur of the rivulet singing its way briskly into the valley.

When the birds took shelter among the boughs, and the flowers folded their petals, and tremendous silence descended, I heard a rustle of feet though the grass. I took heed and saw a young couple approaching my arbor. They sat under a tree where I could see them without being seen.

After he looked about in every direction, I heard the young man saying, "Sit by me, my beloved, and listen to my heart. Smile, for your happiness is a symbol of our future. Be merry, for the sparkling days rejoice with us.

"My soul is warning me of the doubt in your heart, for doubt in love is a sin. Soon you will be the owner of this vast land, lighted by this beautiful moon. Soon you will be the mistress of my palace, and all the servants and maids will obey your commands.

"Smile, my beloved, like the gold smiles from my father's coffers.

"My heart refuses to deny you its secret. Twelve months of comfort and travel await us. For a year we will spend my father's gold at the blue lakes of Switzerland, and viewing the edifices of Italy and Egypt, and resting under the Holy Cedars of Lebanon. You will meet the princesses who will envy you for your jewels and clothes.

"All these things I will do for you. Will you be satisfied?"

In a little while I saw them walking and stepping on flowers as the rich step upon the hearts of the poor.

As they disappeared from my sight, I began to make a comparison between love and money and to analyze their position in the heart. Money!

The source of insincere love, the spring of false light and fortune, the well of poisoned water, the desperation of old age!

I was still wandering in the vast desert of contemplation when a forlorn and spectre-like couple passed by me and sat on the grass: a young man and a young woman who had left their farming shacks in the nearby fields for this cool and solitary place.

After a few moments of complete silence, I heard the following words uttered with sighs from weather-bitten lips.

"Shed not tears, my beloved. Love that opens our eyes and enslaves our hearts can give us the blessing of patience. Be consoled in our delay, for we have taken an oath and entered love's shrine. For our love will ever grow in adversity. For it is in love's name that we are suffering the obstacles of poverty and the sharpness of misery and the emptiness of separation. I shall attack these hardships until I triumph and place in your hands a strength that will help overcome all things to complete the journey of life.

"Love, which is God, will consider our sighs and tears as incense burned at the altar and will reward us with fortitude. Goodbye, my beloved. I must leave before the heartening moon vanishes."

A pure voice, combined of the consuming flame of love, the hopeless bitterness of longing, and the resolved sweetness of patience said, "Good-bye, my beloved."

They separated, and the elegy to their union was smothered by the wails of my crying heart.

I looked upon slumbering nature and with deep reflection discovered the reality of a vast and infinite thing—something no power could demand, influence or acquire, nor riches purchase. Nor could it be effaced by the tears of time or deadened by sorrow—a thing that cannot be discovered by the blue lakes of Switzerland or the beautiful edifices of Italy. It is something that gathers strength with patience, grows despite obstacles, warms in winter, flourishes in spring, casts a breeze in summer, and bears fruit in autumn. I found love.

Love Cleansed by Tears

Hearts that are united through the medium of
  sorrow
will not be separated by the glory of happiness.
Love that is cleansed by tears
will remain eternally pure and beautiful.

A Woman's Heart

Selma told me:

"A woman's heart will not change with time or season. Even if it dies eternally, it will never perish.

"A woman's heart is like a field turned into a battleground. After the trees are uprooted, and the grass is burned, and the rocks are reddened with blood, and the earth is planted with bones and skulls, it is calm and silent as if nothing had happened.

"For the spring and autumn come at their intervals and resume their work."

Love Caresses and Threshes

Even as love crowns you,
so shall it crucify you.
Even as love is for your growth,
so is love for your pruning.
Even as love ascends to your height
and caresses your tenderest branches
that quiver in the sun,
so shall love descend to your roots
and shake them in their clinging to the earth.

Like sheaves of corn
love gathers you unto itself.
Love threshes you to make you naked.
Love sifts you to free you from your husks.
Love grinds you to whiteness.
Love kneads you until you are pliant,
and then love assigns you to its sacred fire,
that you may become
bread for God's sacred feast.

All these things shall love do unto you
that you may know the secrets of your heart,
and in that knowledge
become a fragment of Life's heart.

LOVE'S AUTUMN

Let us go and gather grapes
in the vineyard for the winepress,
and keep the wine in old vases,
as the spirit keeps knowledge of the ages
in eternal vessels.

Let us return to our dwelling,
for the wind has caused the yellow leaves
to fall and shroud the withering flowers
that whisper elegy to summer.

Come home, my eternal sweetheart!
For the birds have made pilgrimage to warmth
and left the chilled prairies
suffering pangs of solitude.
The jasmine and myrtle
have no more tears.

Let us retreat—
for the tired brook has ceased its song,
the bubblesome springs are
drained of their copious weeping,
and the cautious old hills have
stored away their colorful garments.

Come, my beloved!
Nature is justly weary and
is bidding her enthusiasm farewell
with quiet and contented melody.

Between Heart and Soul

A lover speaks about his beloved:

Blame never diverts the heart from its
   purpose,
and loneliness deflects not the soul from the
   truth.

A man between his heart and his soul
is like a tender branch
between the north and south winds.

I am following you, O Love!
What do you seek of me?
I have walked with you
upon the flaming path,
and when I opened my eyes,
I saw naught but darkness.
My lips quivered,
but you let them speak
only words of misery.

Love, you have made my heart hungry
for the sweetness of your presence,
for I am weak and you are strong.
Why are you struggling with me?

The brooks hurry to their lover, the sea.
The flowers smile at their sweetheart, the sun.
The clouds descend to their suitor, the valley.
I am unheard by the brooks,
unseen by the flowers,
unknown to the clouds.

When I discovered that you are a princess,
and I looked upon my poverty,
I learned that God possesses
a secret unrevealed to humanity:
that a secret path leads the spirit to
places where love may forget
the customs of the earth.

When I looked at your eyes,
I knew that this path leads to a paradise
whose door is the human heart.

TEARS AND DEWDROPS

You may forget the one
with whom you have laughed,
but never the one
with whom you have wept.

There must be something strangely sacred
    in salt.
It is in our tears and in the sea.

Our God in His gracious thirst
will drink us all,
the dewdrop and the tear.

DEPTH

Ever has it been that
love knows not its own depth
until the hour of separation.

WHERE ARE YOU NOW,
MY OTHER SELF?

O companion of my soul, where are you?

Do you have a memory of the day we met, when the halo of your spirit surrounded us, and the angels of love floated about us, singing the praise of the soul's deed?

Do you recollect our sitting in the shade of the branches, sheltering ourselves from humanity, as the ribs protect the divine secret of the heart from injury?

Do you remember the trails and forest we walked, with hands joined, and our heads leaning against each other, as if we were hiding ourselves within ourselves?

Do you recall the hour I bade you farewell, and the kiss you placed on my lips? That kiss taught me that joining lips in love reveals heavenly secrets that the tongue cannot utter!

That kiss was an introduction to a great sigh, like the Almighty's breath that turned earth into a human being.

I remember when you kissed me and kissed me, with tears coursing down your cheeks, and you said, "Earthly bodies must often separate for earthly purpose, and must live apart impelled by worldly intent.

"But the spirit remains joined safely in the hands of love, until death arrives and takes joined souls to God.

"Go, my beloved. Love has chosen you her delegate. Obey her, for she is Beauty, who offers to her follower the cup of the sweetness of life."

Where are you now, my other self? Are you awake in the silence of the night? Let the clean breeze convey to you my heart's every beat and affection.

Are you fondling my face in your memory? That image is no longer my own, for sorrow has dropped its shadow on my happy countenance of the past.

Sobs have withered my eyes, which reflected your beauty, and dried my lips, which you sweetened with kisses.

Where are you, my beloved? Do you hear my weeping from beyond the ocean? Do you understand my need? Do you know the greatness of my patience?

Where are you, my beautiful star? The obscurity of life has cast me upon its bosom. Sorrow has conquered me.

Sail your smile into the air. It will reach and enliven me!

Breathe your fragrance into the air. It will sustain me!

Oh, how great is love, and how little am I!

WHO IS CRUCIFYING THE SUN?

Suzannah of Nazareth speaks of Mary, Jesus' mother:

Two Sabbaths ago, my heart was as a stone in my breast, for my son had left me for a ship in Tyre. He would be a sailor. And he said he would return no more.

And upon an evening, I sought Mary.

When I entered her house, she was sitting at her loom, but she was not weaving. She was looking into the sky beyond Nazareth.

And I said to her, "Hail, Mary."

And she stretched out her arm to me and said, "Come and sit beside me, and let us watch the sun pour its blood upon the hills."

I sat beside her on the bench, and we gazed into the west through the window.

And after a moment, Mary said, "I wonder, who is crucifying the sun this eventide?"

Then I said, "I came to you for comfort. My son has left me for the sea and I am alone in the house across the way."

Then Mary said, "I would comfort you, but how shall I?"

And I said, "If you will only speak of your son, I shall be comforted."

And Mary smiled upon me, and she laid her hand about my shoulder and she said, "I will speak of him. That which will console you will give me consolation."

Then she spoke of Jesus, and she spoke long of all that was in the beginning.

And it seemed to me that in her speech she would have no difference between her son and mine.

For she said to me, "My son is also a seafarer. Why would you not trust your son to the waves, even as I have trusted him?

"Woman shall be forever the womb and the cradle, but never the tomb. We die that we may give life unto life, even as our fingers spin the thread for the raiment that we shall never wear.

"And we cast the net for the fish that we shall never taste.

"And for this we sorrow, yet in all this is our joy."

Thus spoke Mary to me.

And I left her and came to my house. And though the light of the day was spent, I sat at my loom to weave more of the cloth.

Seasons of Your Heart

Your pain is the breaking of the shell
that encloses your understanding.

Even as the stone of the fruit must break,
that its heart may stand in the sun,
so must you know pain.

If you could keep your heart in wonder
at the daily miracles of your life,
your pain would not seem
less wondrous than your joy.

You would accept the seasons of your heart,
even as you have always accepted
the seasons that pass over your fields.

GREAT LONGING

The madman speaks:

Here I sit between my brother the mountain and my sister the sea.

We three are one in loneliness, and the love that binds us together is deep and strong and strange. Nay, it is deeper than my sister's depth and stronger than my brother's strength, and stranger than the strangeness of my madness.

Aeons upon aeons have passed since the first grey dawn made us visible to one another. And though we have seen the birth and the fullness and the death of many worlds, we are still eager and young.

We are young and eager, and yet we are mateless and unvisited. And though we lie in unbroken half-embrace, we are uncomforted. And what comfort is there for controlled desire and unspent passion? Whence shall come the flaming god to warm my sister's bed? And what she-torrent shall quench my brother's fire? And who is the woman that shall command my heart?

In the stillness of the night, my sister murmurs in her sleep the fire-god's unknown name, and my brother calls afar upon the cool and distant goddess. But upon whom I call in my sleep, I know not.

Here I sit between my brother the mountain and my sister the sea. We three are one in loneliness, and the love that binds us together is deep and strong and strange.

LONGING BEYOND WORDS

We were fluttering, wandering,
longing creatures
a thousand thousand years
before the sea and the wind in the forest
gave us words.

Now, how can we express
the ancient of days in us
with only the sounds
of our yesterdays?

The Sphinx spoke only once,
and the Sphinx said,
"A grain of sand is a desert,
and a desert is a grain of sand.
And now let us all be silent again."

Alone?

Alone?
And what of it?
You came alone,
and alone shall you
pass into the mist.

Therefore drink your cup
alone and in silence.

The autumn days have given
other lips other cups and
filled them with wine,
bitter and sweet,
even as they have
filled your cup.

Drink your cup alone
though it tastes of
your own blood and tears,
and praise life for
the gift of thirst.

For without thirst
your heart is but
the shore of a barren sea,
songless and without a tide.

Unsealing the Heart

How shall my heart be unsealed
unless it be broken?
Only great sorrow or great joy
can reveal your truth.
If you would be revealed
you must either
dance naked in the sun
or carry your cross.

Speaking and Listening
to the Heart

The voice of life in me cannot
reach the ear of life in you,
but let us talk that
we may not feel lonely.

Should one tell a lie that
does not hurt you nor anyone else,
why not say in your heart
that the house of facts
is too small for his fancies,
and he had to leave it
for a larger space?

A great person has two hearts:
one bleeds and the other forbears.

The reality of other people is
not in what they reveal to you,
but in what they cannot reveal to you.

Therefore if you would understand them,
listen not to what they say
but rather to what they do not say.

Freedom and Slavery

You are free before the sun of the day
and free before the stars of the night.
And you are free when there are
no sun and no moon and no stars.

You are even free when
you close your eyes
upon all there is.

But you are a slave to
the one whom you love
because you love him,
And a slave to her
who loves you
because she loves you.

If you would possess,
you must not claim.

WEEP FOR THE BELOVED. . . .

The woman of Byblos offers a lamentation at the time of Jesus[2]:

Weep with me, ye daughters of Astarte,
and all ye lovers of Tammuz.

Bid your heart melt and rise
and run with blood-tears,
for he who was made of gold and ivory
is no more.

---

2. Byblos (now called Jubayl) was an ancient city on the Mediterranean coast in present day Lebanon. Previously occupied by Egypt and Assyria, Byblos is associated with Great Goddess Astarte (called "the Lady of Byblos") and her dying god consort Tammuz. The worship of both was undoubtedly still strong at the time of Jesus.

In the dark forest, the boar overcame him,
and the tusks of the boar pierced his flesh.
Now he lies stained with the
    leaves of yesteryear,
and no longer shall his footsteps wake the seeds
that sleep in the bosom of the spring.

His voice will not come
with the dawn to my window,
and I shall be forever alone.

Weep with me, ye daughters of Astarte,
and all ye lovers of Tammuz,
for my beloved has escaped me.

He who spoke as the rivers speak,
he whose voice and time were twins,
he whose mouth was a red pain made sweet,
he on whose lips gall would turn to honey.

Weep with me, daughters of Astarte,
and ye lovers of Tammuz!

Weep with me around his bier
as the stars weep and
as the moon-petals fall
upon his wounded body.
Wet with your tears
the silken covers of my bed,
where my beloved
once lay in my dream
and was gone away
in my awakening.

I charge ye, daughters of Astarte,
and all ye lovers of Tammuz!

Bare your breasts and weep and comfort me,
for Jesus of Nazareth is dead.

Harvesting the Heart's Pain

A poet's voice speaks:

The power of charity sows seed deep in my heart, and I reap and gather the wheat in bundles and give it to the hungry.

My soul gives life to the grapevine, and I press its bunches and give the juice to the thirsty.

Heaven fills my lamp with oil, and I place it at my window to direct the stranger through the dark.

I do all these things because I live in them. And if destiny should tie my hands and prevent me from so doing, then death would be my only desire. For I am a poet, and if I cannot give, I shall refuse to receive.

Humanity rages like a tempest, but I sigh in silence for I know the storm must pass away, while a sigh goes to God.

Humanity clings to earthly things, but I seek ever to embrace the torch of love so it will purify me by its fire and sear inhumanity from my heart.

Material things deaden people who try to live without suffering. Love awakens them with enlivening pains.

Humanity is divided into different clans and tribes and belongs to countries and towns. But I find myself a stranger to all communities and belong to no settlement.

The universe is my country and the human family is my tribe.

People are weak, and it is sad that they divide among themselves. The world is narrow, and it is unwise to cleave it into kingdoms, empires, and provinces.

Humanity unites itself only to destroy the temples of the soul, and it joins hands to build edifices for earthly bodies.

I stand alone, listening to the voice of hope in my deep self saying, "As love enlivens our heart with pain, so ignorance teaches us the way of knowledge."

Pain and ignorance lead to great joy and knowledge, because the Supreme Being has created nothing vain under the sun.

3

All Our Relationships

Love has many faces, many ways to play
hide and seek. Those whom we call
family, friends, strangers, and enemies
all reveal the fingers of one loving hand.

MOTHER

The most beautiful word on the lips of humanity is the word *mother*. And the most beautiful call is the call of "my mother!" It is a word full of hope and love, a sweet and kind word coming from the depths of the heart.

The mother is everything—she is our consolation in sorrow, our hope in misery, and our strength in weakness. She is the source of love, mercy, sympathy, and forgiveness.

Everything in nature speaks of the mother. The sun is the mother of earth and gives it its nourishment of heat. It never leaves the universe at night until it has put the earth to sleep, to the song of the sea and the hymn of birds and brooks.

And this earth is the mother of trees and flowers. It produces them, nurses them, and weans them. The trees and flowers become kind mothers of their great fruits and seeds. And the mother, the prototype of all existence, is the eternal spirit, full of beauty and love.

The word *mother* is hidden in our hearts, and it comes upon our lips in hours of sorrow and happiness, just as the perfume comes from the heart of the rose and mingles with both clear and cloudy air.

THE SONG THAT LIES SILENT

The song that lies silent
in the heart of a mother
sings upon the lips of her child.
No longing remains unfulfilled.

SAYINGS ON CHILDREN

Long were you a dream in your mother's sleep,
and then she awoke to give you birth.

The germ of the race is in your mother's
    longing.

My father and mother desired a child and they
    begot me.
And I wanted a mother and a father and I begot
    night and the sea.

Some of our children are our justifications and
    some are but our regrets.

LULLABIES

We often sing lullabies to our children
that we ourselves may sleep.

If Love Were in the Flesh . . .

The mother of Judas speaks:

If love were in the flesh
I would burn it out
with hot irons
and be at peace.

But it is in the soul,
unreachable.

HIDE AND SEEK

Now let us play hide and seek.

Should you hide in my heart
it would not be difficult to find you.

But should you hide behind
your own shell,
then it would be useless
for anyone to seek you.

LOVE SONG

A poet once wrote a love song, and it was beautiful. He made many copies of it and sent them to his friends and acquaintances, both men and women, and even to a young woman whom he had met but once, who lived beyond the mountains.

In a day or two, a messenger came from the young woman bringing a letter. And in the letter she said, "Let me assure you, I am deeply touched by the love song that you have written to me. Come now, and see my father and my mother, and we shall make arrangements for the betrothal."

The poet answered the letter and said to her, "My friend, it was but a song of love out of a poet's heart, sung by every man to every woman."

And she wrote again to him saying, "Hypocrite and liar in words! From this day until my coffin-day, I shall hate all poets for your sake."

Love and Hate

A woman said to a man, "I love you."

And the man said, "It is in my heart to be worthy of your love."

And the woman said, "You love me not?"

And the man only gazed upon her and said nothing.

Then the woman cried aloud, "I hate you!"

And the man said, "Then it is also in my heart to be worthy of your hate."

TWO SIDES

Yestereve, on the marble steps of the temple,
I saw a woman sitting between two men.

One side of her face was pale,
the other was blushing.

The Hermit, the Beasts, and Love

Once there lived a hermit among the green hills. He was pure of spirit and white of heart. And all the animals of the land and all the fowl of the air came to him in pairs and he spoke to them. They heard him gladly, and they would gather near him and would not go until nightfall, when he would send them away, entrusting them to the wind and the woods with his blessing.

Upon an evening, as he was speaking of love, a leopard raised her head and said to the hermit, "You speak to us of loving. Tell us, sir, where is your mate?"

And the hermit said, "I have no mate."

Then a great cry of surprise rose from the company of beasts and fowl, and they began to say among themselves, "How can he tell us of loving and mating when he himself knows naught thereof?" And quietly and in disdain they left him alone.

That night the hermit lay upon his mat with his face earthward, and he wept bitterly and beat his hands upon his breast.

WORKING WITH LOVE

What is it to work with love?

It is to weave the cloth with threads drawn from your heart, even as if your beloved were to wear that cloth.

It is to build a house with affection, even as if your beloved were to dwell in that house.

It is to sow seeds with tenderness and reap the harvest with joy, even as if your beloved were to eat the fruit.

It is to charge all things you fashion with a breath of your own spirit.

And to know that all the blessed dead are standing about you watching.

Wave a Bit Nearer. . . .

One branch in bloom said to its neighboring branch, "This is a dull and empty day." And the other branch answered, "It is indeed empty and dull."

At that moment, a sparrow alighted on one of the branches, and then another sparrow nearby.

One of the sparrows chirped and said, "My mate has left me."

And the other sparrow cried, "My mate has also gone, and she will not return. So what do I care?"

Then the two birds began to twitter and scold, and soon they were fighting and making harsh noises upon the air.

All of a sudden, two other sparrows came sailing from the sky and sat quietly beside the restless two. And there was calm, and there was peace.

Then the four flew away together in pairs.

And the first branch said to its neighboring branch, "That was a mighty zig-zag of sound!"

And the other branch answered, "Call it what you will, it is now both peaceful and spacious. And if the upper air makes peace it seems to me that those who dwell in the lower might make peace also. Will you not wave in the wind a little nearer to me?"

And the first branch said, "O perchance, for peace's sake, before the spring is over!"

And then it waved itself with the strong wind to embrace the other.

SAYINGS ON ENEMIES

I have no enemies, O God,
but if I am to have an enemy
let his strength be equal to mine,
that truth alone may be the victor.

You will be quite friendly
with your enemy
when you both die.

Oftentimes I have hated in self-defence.
But if I were stronger,
I would not have used such a weapon.

FRIENDS AND STRANGERS

Georgus of Beruit speaks of Jesus:

He and his friends were in the grove of pines beyond my hedge, and he was talking to them. I stood near the hedge and listened. And I knew who he was, for his fame had reached these shores before he himself visited them.

When he ceased speaking, I approached him and said, "Sir, come with these men and honor me and my roof."

And he smiled upon me and said, "Not this day, my friend. Not this day."

There was a blessing in his words, and his voice enfolded me like a garment on a cold night.

Then he turned to his friends and said, "Behold a man who deems us not strangers, and though he has not seen us ere this day, he bids us to his threshold.

"Verily, in my kingdom there are no strangers. Our life is but the life of all other people, given us that we may know all people and, in that knowledge, love them.

"The deeds of all people are but our deeds, both the hidden and the revealed.

"I charge you not to be one self but rather many selves, the householder and the homeless, the plougher and the sparrow that picks the grain before it slumbers in the earth, the giver who gives in gratitude and the receiver who receives in pride and recognition.

"The beauty of the day is not only in what you see, but in what others see.

"For this I have chosen you from among the many who have chosen me."

Then he turned to me again and smiled and said, "I say these things to you also, and you also shall remember them."

Then I entreated him and said, "Master, will you not visit in my house?"

And he answered, "I know your heart, and I have visited your larger house."

And as he walked away with his disciples he said, "Good night, and may your house be large enough to shelter all the wanderers of the land."

FRIENDSHIP—HOURS TO LIVE

When your friend speaks his mind, you fear not the "nay" in your own mind, nor do you withhold the "aye."

And when your friend is silent, your heart ceases not to listen to his heart.

For without words, in friendship all thoughts, all desires, and all expectations are born and shared with a joy that is unacclaimed.

When you part from your friend you grieve not, for that which you love most in him may be clearer in his absence, as the mountain to the climber is clearer from the plain.

And let there be no purpose in friendship save the deepening of the spirit.

For love that seeks anything but the disclosure of its own mystery is not love but a net cast forth. And only the unprofitable is caught.

And let your best be for your friend.

If he must know the ebb of your tide, let him know its flood also.

For what is your friend that you should seek him with hours to kill?

Seek him always with hours to live.

Friendship's Sweet Responsibility

Friendship is always a sweet responsibility,
never an opportunity.

If you do not understand your friend
under all conditions
you will never understand him.

LOVING THE NEIGHBOR

When you enjoy loving your neighbour
it ceases to be a virtue.

Your Neighbor Is Your
Unknown Self

Joseph of Arimathea remembers Jesus:

And he would say, "Your neighbour is your unknown self, made visible. His face shall be reflected in your still waters, and if you gaze therein you shall behold your own countenance.

"Should you listen in the night, you shall hear him speak, and his words shall be the throbbing of your own heart.

"Be unto him that which you would have him be unto you.

"This is my law, and I shall say it unto you and unto your children and they unto their children until time is spent and generations are no more."

And on another day he said, "You shall not be yourself alone. You are in the deeds of others, and they, though unknowing, are with you all your days.

"They shall not commit a crime and your hand not be with their hand.

"They shall not fall down but that you shall also fall down. And they shall not rise but that you shall rise with them.

"Their road to the sanctuary is your road, and when they seek the wasteland, you too seek it with them.

"You and your neighbour are two seeds sown in the field. Together you grow, and together you shall sway in the wind. And neither of you shall claim the field. For a seed on its way to growth claims not even its own ecstasy.

"Today I am with you. Tomorrow I go westward. But before I go, I say unto you that your neighbour is your unknown self, made visible.

"Seek him in love that you may know yourself, for only in that knowledge shall you become my brothers."

THE NEIGHBOR UNBEFRIENDED

The space that lies between you and
your near neighbour, unbefriended,
is indeed greater than that which lies between
you and your beloved
who dwells beyond
the seven lands and seven seas.

Your Neighbor Is a Field

Peter recollects his time with Jesus:

Once in Capernaum my lord and master spoke thus:

"Your neighbor is your other self, dwelling behind a wall. In understanding, all walls shall fall down.

"Who knows but that your neighbor is your better self, wearing another body? See that you love him as you would love yourself.

"He too is a manifestation of the Most High, whom you do not know.

"Your neighbor is a field where the springs of your hope walk in their green garments, and where the winters of your desire dream of snowy heights.

"Your neighbor is a mirror wherein you shall behold your countenance made beautiful by a joy which you yourself did not know and by a sorrow you yourself did not share.

"I would have you love your neighbor even as I have loved you."

Then I asked him saying, "How can I love a neighbor who loves me not and who covets my property? One who would steal my possessions?"

And he answered, "When you are ploughing and your servant is sowing the seed behind you, would you stop and look backward and put to flight a sparrow feeding upon a few of your seeds? Should you do this, you were not worthy of the riches of your harvest."

When Jesus had said this, I was ashamed and I was silent. But I was not in fear, for he smiled upon me.

Love and Patriotism

A poet's voice speaks:

I have a yearning for my beautiful country, and I love its people because of their misery. But if my people rose, stimulated by plunder and motivated by what they call "patriotic spirit," to murder and invade my neighbor's country, then upon the committing of any human atrocity, I would hate my people and my country.

I sing the praise of my birthplace and long to see the home of my children. But if the people in that home refused to shelter and feed the needy wayfarer, I would convert my praise to anger and my longing to forgetfulness. My inner voice would say, "The house that does not comfort the needy is worthy of nothing but destruction."

I love my native village with some of my love for my country. And I love my country with part of my love for the earth, all of which is my country. And I love the earth with all of myself, because it is the haven of humanity, the manifest spirit of God.

Humanity is the spirit of the Supreme Being on earth, and that humanity is standing amidst ruins, hiding its nakedness behind tattered rags, shedding tears upon hollow cheeks, and calling for its children with a pitiful voice. But the children are busy singing their clan's anthem. They are busy sharpening the swords and cannot hear the cry of their mothers.

Humanity appeals to its people but they listen not. Were one to listen and console a mother by wiping her tears, others would say, "He is weak, affected by sentiment."

Humanity is the spirit of the Supreme Being on earth, and that Supreme Being preaches love and good will. But the people ridicule such teachings. The Nazarene Jesus listened, and crucifixion was his lot. Socrates heard the voice and followed it, and he too fell victim in body. The followers of the Nazarene and Socrates are the followers of deity, and since people will not kill them, they deride them saying, "Ridicule is more bitter than killing."

Jerusalem could not kill the Nazarene, nor Athens Socrates. They are living yet and shall live eternally. Ridicule cannot triumph over the followers of deity. They live and grow forever.

Spaces in Your Togetherness

You were born together and
together you shall be forevermore.

But let there be spaces in your togetherness,
and let the winds of the heavens
dance between you.

Love one another
but make not a bond of love.
Let it rather be a moving sea
between the shores of your souls.

Sing and dance together and be joyous,
but let each one of you be alone,
even as the strings of a lute are alone
though they quiver with the same music.

Give your hearts, but not into each other's
    keeping.
For only the hand of Life can contain your
    hearts.

Flame to Flame

[The ancient Earth Gods continue their conversation about the purpose of life while observing a loving couple embracing each other:]

Behold, man and woman,
flame to flame in white ecstasy.
Roots that suck at the breast of purple earth,
flame flowers at the breasts of the sky.
And we are the purple breast,
And we are the enduring sky.

Our soul, even the soul of life,
your soul and mine,
dwells this night in a throat enflamed,
and garments the body of a girl with beating
    waves.

Your sceptre cannot sway this destiny,
your weariness is but ambition.
This and all is wiped away
in the passion of a man and a maid.

They who are conquered by love,
and upon whose bodies
love's chariot ran from sea to mountain
and again from mountain to the sea,
stand even now in a shy half-embrace.

Petal to petal
they breathe the sacred perfume.
Soul to soul
they find the soul of life.
And upon their eyelids
lies a prayer
unto you and unto me.

Love is a night bent down
to a bower anointed,
a sky turned meadow,
and all the stars turned to fireflies.

True it is, we are the beyond,
and we are the most high.

But love is beyond our questioning,
and love outsoars our song.

LOVING THE LOST SHEEP

A shepherd in southern Lebanon speaks about meeting Jesus:

Then he said, and there was joy and laughter in his voice, "Let us go into the North Country and meet the spring.

"Come with me to the hills, for winter is past and the snows of Lebanon are descending to the valleys to sing with the brooks.

"The fields and the vineyards have banished sleep and are awake to greet the sun with their green figs and tender grapes."

It was late summer when he and three other men first walked upon that road yonder. It was evening, and he stopped and stood there at the end of the pasture.

I was playing upon my flute, and my flock was grazing all around me. When he stopped, I rose and walked over and stood before him.

And he asked me, "Where is the grave of Elijah? Is it not somewhere near this place?"

And I answered him, "It is there, sir, underneath that great heap of stones. Even unto this day every passerby brings a stone and places it upon the heap."

He thanked me and walked away, and his friends walked behind him.

After three days Gamaliel, who was also a shepherd, said to me that the man who had passed by was a prophet in Judea. But I did not believe him. Yet I thought of that man for many a moon.

When spring came, Jesus passed once more by this pasture, and this time he was alone.

I was not playing on my flute that day, for I had lost a sheep and was bereaved. And my heart was downcast within me.

I walked towards him and stood still before him, for I desired to be comforted.

And he looked at me and said, "You do not play upon your flute this day. Whence is the sorrow in your eyes?"

I answered, "A sheep from among my sheep is lost. I have sought her everywhere but I find her not. And I know not what to do."

He was silent for a moment. Then he smiled upon me and said, "Wait here awhile and I will find your sheep." And he walked away and disappeared among the hills.

After an hour he returned, and my sheep was close behind him. As he stood before me, the sheep looked up into his face even as I was looking. Then I embraced her in gladness.

And he put his hand upon my shoulder and said, "From this day you shall love this sheep more than any other in your flock, for she was lost and now she is found."

And again I embraced my sheep in gladness, and she came close to me, and I was silent.

But when I raised my head to thank Jesus, he was already walking afar off, and I had not the courage to follow Him.

THE FINGERS OF ONE LOVING HAND

A poet's voice speaks:

You are my brother and sister, because you are human beings. We are all children of one Holy Spirit. We are equal and made of the same earth.

You are here as my companions along the path of life and my aid in understanding the meaning of hidden truth.

You are human beings, and that fact sufficing, I love you. You may speak of me as you choose, for tomorrow shall take you away and will use your talk as evidence for its judgment. And you shall receive justice.

You may deprive me of whatever I possess. For my greed instigated the amassing of wealth, and you are entitled to my lot if it will satisfy you.

You may do unto me whatever you wish, but you shall not be able to touch my truth.

You may shed my blood and burn my body, but you cannot kill or hurt my spirit.

You may tie my hands with chains and my feet with shackles and put me in the dark prison. But you shall not enslave my thinking, for it is free like the breeze in the spacious sky.

You are my brother and sister and I love you. I love you worshipping in your church, kneeling in your temple, and praying in your mosque. You and I and all are children of one religion, for the varied paths of religion are but the fingers of the loving hand of the Supreme Being, extended to all, offering completeness of spirit to all, anxious to receive all.

I love you for your truth, derived from your knowledge, that truth which I cannot see because of my ignorance. But I respect it as a divine thing, for it is the deed of the spirit. Your truth shall meet my truth in the coming world and blend together like the fragrance of flowers. It shall become one whole and eternal truth, perpetuating and living in the eternity of love and beauty.

I love you because you are weak before the strong oppressor, and poor before the greedy rich. For these reasons I shed tears and comfort you.

And from behind my tears I see you embraced in the arms of justice, smiling and forgiving your persecutors.

You are my brother and sister, and I love you.

4

A Love Beyond

Love is more than an emotion. It is a
sacred force that breaks our ideas of
who we think we are and transports us
on a path that extends through this life
and beyond.

LOVE'S WINTER

Come close to me,
O companion of my full life!

Come close to me,
and let not winter's touch
enter between us.

Sit by me before the hearth,
for fire is the only fruit of winter.

Speak to me of the glory of your heart,
for that is greater than
the shrieking elements beyond our door.

Bind the door and seal the transoms,
for the angry countenance of the heaven
depresses my spirit,
and the face of our snow-laden fields
makes my soul cry.

Feed the lamp with oil
and let it not dim,
and place it by you,
so I can read with tears what
your life with me has
written upon your face.

Bring autumn's wine!
Let us drink and sing
the song of remembrance
to spring's carefree sowing
and summer's watchful tending
and autumn's reward in harvest.

Come close to me,
O beloved of my soul!
The fire is cooling and fleeing
under the ashes.

Embrace me,
for I fear loneliness.
The lamp is dim,
and the wine that we pressed
is closing our eyes.
Let us look upon each other
before they are shut.

Find me with your arms and embrace me.
Let slumber then embrace our souls as one.

Kiss me, my beloved,
for winter has stolen
all but our moving lips.

You are close by me, my forever.

How deep and wide will be
the ocean of slumber.
And how recent was the dawn!

A RHYTHM FOR LOVERS

You shall rise beyond your words,
but your path shall remain
a rhythm and a fragrance—
a rhythm for lovers
and for all who are beloved,
and a fragrance for those who would
live life in a garden.

You shall go down deeper
than your words, aye,
deeper than all sounds,
to the very heart of the earth.
And there you shall be alone
with the One who walks
upon the Milky Way.

LOVE IS THE ONLY FREEDOM

Love is the only freedom in the world
because it so elevates the spirit
that the laws of humanity and
the phenomena of nature
do not alter its course.

LOVE IS JUSTICE

A poet's voice speaks:

You are my brothers and sisters, but why are you quarrelling with me? Why do you invade my country and try to subjugate me for the sake of pleasing those who are seeking glory and authority?

Why do you leave your wives, husbands and children and follow death to a distant land for the sake of those who buy glory with your blood and high honor with your mothers' tears?

Is it an honor for a man to kill his brother? If you deem it an honor, let it be an act of worship and erect a temple to Cain, who slew his brother Abel.

Is self-preservation the first law of nature? Why then does greed urge you to self-sacrifice in order only to achieve its aim in hurting your brothers and sisters? Beware, my brothers and sisters, of the leader who says, "Love of existence obliges us to deprive the people of their rights!"

I say unto you but this:

Protecting others' rights is the noblest and most beautiful human act. If my existence requires that I kill others, then death is more honorable to me. And if I cannot find someone to kill me for the protection of my honor, I will not hesitate to take my life by my own hands for the sake of eternity, before eternity comes.

Selfishness, my brothers and sisters, is the cause of blind superiority, and superiority creates clanship, and clanship creates authority that leads to discord and subjugation.

The soul believes in the power of knowledge and justice over dark ignorance. It denies the authority that supplies the swords to defend and strengthen ignorance and oppression. That authority destroyed Babylon and shook the foundations of Jerusalem and left Rome in ruins. It is that which made people call criminals great, made writers respect their names, and made historians relate the stories of their inhumanity in the manner of praise.

The only authority I obey is the knowledge of guarding and acquiescing in the natural law of justice. What justice does authority display when it kills the killer? When it imprisons the robber? When it descends on a neighbor country and slays its people?

What does justice think of the authority under which a killer punishes the one who kills, and a thief sentences the one who steals?

You are my brothers and sisters, and I love you. And love is justice with its full intensity and dignity. If justice did not support my love for you, regardless of your tribe and community, I would be a deceiver, concealing the ugliness of selfishness behind the outer garment of pure love.

Silence Whispers to the Heart

It is not the syllables that come from lips and tongues that bring hearts together. There is something greater and purer than what the mouth utters.

Silence illuminates our souls, whispers to our hearts, and brings them together.

Silence separates us from ourselves, makes us sail the firmament of spirit, and brings us closer to heaven.

It makes us feel that bodies are no more than prisons, and that this world is only a place of exile.

LOVE SONG OF THE WAVE

The strong shore is my beloved,
and I am his sweetheart.

We are at last united by love,
and then the moon draws me from him.

I go to him in haste and
depart reluctantly,
with many little farewells.

I steal swiftly from
behind the blue horizon
to cast the silver of my foam
upon the gold of his sand,
and we blend in melted brilliance.

I quench his thirst and submerge his heart.
He softens my voice and subdues my temper.

At dawn I recite the rules of love to his ears,
and he embraces me longingly.

At eventide I sing to him the song of hope,
and then print smooth kisses on his face.

I am swift and fearful,
but he is quiet, patient, and thoughtful.
His broad bosom soothes my restlessness.

As the tide comes, we caress each other.
When it withdraws, I drop to his feet in prayer.

Many times have I danced around mermaids
as they rose from the depths
and rested upon my crest
to watch the stars.

Many times have I heard lovers
complain of their smallness,
and I helped them to sigh.

Many times have I teased the great rocks
and fondled them with a smile,
but never have I received
laughter from them.

Many times have I lifted drowning souls
and carried them tenderly
to my beloved shore.
He gives them strength
as he takes mine.

Many times have I stolen
gems from the depths and
presented them to my beloved shore.
He takes them in silence,
but still I give,
for he welcomes me ever.

In the heaviness of night,
when all creatures seek
the ghost of slumber,
I sit up, singing at one time
and sighing at another.
I am awake always.

Alas! Sleeplessness has weakened me!

But I am a lover,
and the truth of love is strong.
I may be weary,
but I shall never die.

SEEDS OF HEART

Every seed is a longing.

Sow a seed and
the earth will yield you a flower.

Dream your dream to the sky
and it will bring you your beloved.

SONG OF LOVE

I am the lover's eyes
and the spirit's wine
and the heart's nourishment.

I am a rose—
my heart opens at dawn and
the virgin kisses me and
places me upon her breast.

I am the house of true fortune
and the origin of pleasure
and the beginning of peace and tranquillity.

I am the gentle smile upon the lips of beauty.

When youth overtakes me
he forgets his toil,
and his whole life becomes
a reality of sweet dreams.

KAHLIL GIBRAN'S LITTLE BOOK OF LOVE

I am the poet's elation
and the artist's revelation
and the musician's inspiration.

I am a sacred shrine
in the heart of a child
adored by a merciful mother.

I appear to a heart's cry.
I shun a demand.
My fullness pursues the heart's desire.
It shuns the empty claim of the voice.

I appeared to Adam through Eve
and exile was their lot.
Yet I revealed myself to Solomon,
and he drew wisdom from my presence.

I smiled at Helena, and she destroyed Tarwada[3].
Yet I crowned Cleopatra and
peace dominated the Valley of the Nile.

---

3. Arabic for Troy.

I am like the ages—
building today and destroying tomorrow.
I am like a god who creates and ruins.

I am sweeter than a violet's sigh.
I am more violent than a raging tempest.

Gifts alone do not entice me,
parting does not discourage me,
poverty does not chase me,
jealousy does not prove my awareness,
madness does not evidence my presence.

O seekers, I am truth
beseeching truth.
And your truth in
seeking and receiving
and protecting me
shall determine my behavior.

LOVE'S LIGHT

Love is a word of light,
written by a hand of light,
upon a page of light.

LOVE IS SUFFICIENT TO ITSELF

Love gives naught but itself
and takes naught but from itself.
Love possesses not
nor would it be possessed.

For love is sufficient unto love.

When you love, you should not say
"God is in my heart," but rather
"I am in the heart of God."

When Love Becomes Vast

Looking back, John of Patmos speaks of Jesus:

Once more I would speak of him.

God gave me the voice and the burning lips though not the speech. And unworthy am I for the fuller word, yet I would summon my heart to my lips.

Jesus loved me, and I knew not why. And I loved him because he quickened my spirit to heights beyond my stature and to depths beyond my sounding.

Love is a sacred mystery.
To those who love,
it remains forever wordless.
But to those who do not love,
it may be but a heartless jest.

Jesus called me and my brother when we were laboring in the field. I was young then, and only the voice of dawn had visited my ears.

But his voice and the trumpet of his voice was the end of my labor and the beginning of my passion. And there were nothing for me then but to walk in the sun and worship the loveliness of the hour.

Could you conceive a majesty too kind to be majestic?

And a beauty too radiant to seem beautiful?

Could you hear in your dreams a voice shy of its own rapture?

He called me and I followed Him.

That evening I returned to my father's house to get my other cloak. And I said to my mother, "Jesus of Nazareth would have me in his company."

And she said, "Go his way my son, even like your brother." And I accompanied him. His fragrance called me and commanded me, but only to release me.

Love is a gracious host to its guests,
though to the unbidden
its house is a mirage and a mockery.

Now you would have me explain the miracles of Jesus.

We are all the miraculous gesture of the moment. Our lord and master was the centre of that moment. Yet it was not in his desire that his gestures be known.

I have heard him say to the lame, "Rise and go home, but say not to the priest that I have made you whole."

And Jesus's mind was not with the cripple. It was rather with the strong and the upright. His mind sought and held other minds, and his complete spirit visited other spirits. And in so doing his spirit changed these minds and these spirits.

It seemed miraculous, but with our lord and master it was simply like breathing the air of every day.

And now let me speak of other things.

On a day when he and I were alone walking in a field, we were both hungry, and we came to a wild apple tree. There were only two apples hanging on the bough. And he held the trunk of the tree with his arm and shook it, and the two apples fell down.

He picked them both up and gave one to me. The other he held in his hand. In my hunger I ate the apple, and I ate it fast.

Then I looked at him, and I saw that he still held the other apple in his hand. And he gave it to me saying, "Eat this also."

And I took the apple, and in my shameless hunger I ate it. And as we walked on I looked upon His face. But how shall I tell you of what I saw?

A night where candles burn in space . . .
a dream beyond our reaching . . .
a noon where all shepherds are at peace and
happy that their flock are grazing . . .
an eventide, and a stillness, and a
     homecoming . . .
then a sleep and a dream.

KAHLIL GIBRAN'S LITTLE BOOK OF LOVE

All these things I saw in His face.

He had given me the two apples. And I knew he was hungry even as I was hungry. But I now know that in giving them to me he had been satisfied. He himself ate of other fruit from another tree.

I would tell you more of him, but how shall I?

When love becomes vast,
love becomes wordless.
And when memory is overladen
it seeks the silent deep.

OUT OF MY DEEPER HEART

Out of my deeper heart
a bird rose and flew skywards.
Higher and higher did it rise,
yet larger and larger did it grow.
At first it was but like a swallow,
then a lark, then an eagle,
then as vast as a spring cloud,
and then it filled the starry heavens.
Out of my heart a bird flew skywards,
and it waxed larger as it flew.
Yet it left not my heart.

O my faith,
my untamed knowledge!
How shall I fly to your height,
and see with you our larger self
pencilled upon the sky?
How shall I turn this sea within me into mist
and move with you in space immeasurable?
How can a prisoner within the temple
behold its golden domes?
How shall the heart of a fruit
be stretched to envelop the fruit also?

O my faith!
I am in chains behind these bars
of silver and ebony,
and I cannot fly with you.
Yet out of my heart you rise skyward,
and it is my heart that holds you,
and I shall be content.

Longing for the Heart
of the Beloved

Lazarus laments being brought back to life by Jesus and speaks to his sister, Mary of Bethany. A madman listens nearby and comments.

Lazarus:

I was a stream and I sought the sea
where my beloved dwells.
And when I reached the sea,
I was brought to the hills
to run again among the rocks.

I was a song imprisoned in silence,
longing for the heart of my beloved.
And when the winds of heaven released me
and uttered me in that green forest,
I was recaptured by a voice,
and I was turned again into silence.

I was a root in the dark earth,
and I became a flower
and then a fragrance in space rising
to enfold my beloved,
and then I was caught and
gathered by hand,
and I was made a root again,
a root in the dark earth.

The Madman:

If you are a root,
you can always escape
the tempests in the branches.
And it is good to be a running stream
even after you have reached the sea.
Of course it is good for water
to run upward.

Mary:

But my brother!
It is good to be a running stream,
and it is not good to be a song not yet sung,
and it is good to be a root in the dark earth.

The Master knew all this
and he called you back to us
that we may know there is
no veil between life and death.
Do you not see how
one word uttered in love
may bring together elements
scattered by an illusion called death?

Believe and have faith,
for only in faith,
which is our deeper knowledge,
can you find comfort.

Lazarus:

Comfort?
Comfort, the treacherous, the deadly!
Comfort that cheats our senses and
makes us slaves to the passing hour!
I would not have comfort.
I would have passion!
I would burn in the cool space
with my beloved.
I would be in the boundless space
with my mate, my other self.

O Mary, Mary, you were once my sister,
and we knew one another even
when our nearest kin knew us not.
Now listen to me, listen to me with your heart.

We were in space, my beloved and I,
and we were all space.
We were in light
and we were all light.
And we roamed even like the ancient spirit
that moved upon the face of the waters,
and it was forever the first day.

We were love itself that dwells
in the heart of the white silence.
Then a voice like thunder,
a voice like countless spears
piercing the ether, cried out saying,
"Lazarus, come forth!"

And the voice echoed and
re-echoed in space
and I, even as a flood tide,
became an ebbing tide.
A house divided, a garment rent,
a youth unspent, a tower that fell down,
and out of its broken stones
a landmark was made.

A voice cried "Lazarus, come forth!"
And I descended from
the mansion of the sky to
a tomb within a tomb,
this body in a sealed cave.

LOVE AND TIME

Who among you does not feel that
your power to love is boundless?

And yet who does not feel
that very love, though boundless,
encompassed within the center of your being?
Yet moving not from love-thought to love-
    thought,
nor from love-deeds to other love-deeds.

And is not time, even as love is,
undivided and paceless?

But if in thought
you must measure
time into seasons,
let each season
encircle all the other seasons,
and let today
embrace the past with remembrance
and the future with longing.

LOVE CREATED IN A MOMENT

It is wrong to think that love comes
from long companionship
and persevering courtship.

Love is the offspring of spiritual affinity,
and unless that affinity
is created in a moment,
it will not be created
in years or even generations.

THE GARDENS OF OUR PASSION

Thirty years later, Mary Magdalene reflects:

Once again I say that, with death Jesus con-
quered death and rose from the grave a spirit
and a power. And he walked in our solitude and
visited the gardens of our passion.

He lies not there in that cleft rock behind
the stone.

We who love him beheld him with these our
eyes, which he made to see. And we touched
him with these our hands, which he taught to
reach forth.

I know you who believe not in him. I was
one of you, and you are many. But your number
shall be diminished.

Must you break your harp and your lyre to
find the music therein?

Or must you fell a tree ere you can believe
it bears fruit?

You hate Jesus because someone from the North Country said he was the son of God. But you hate one another, because each of you deems himself too great to be the brother of the next one.

You hate him because someone said he was born of a virgin, and not of human seed.

But you know not the mothers who go to the tomb in virginity, nor the men who go down to the grave choked with their own thirst.

You know not that the earth was given in marriage to the sun, and that earth it is who sends us forth to the mountain and the desert.

There is a gulf that yawns between those who love him and those who hate him, between those who believe and those who do not believe.

But when the years have bridged that gulf, you shall know that he who lived in us is death-less, that he was the son of God even as we are the children of God. That he was born of a virgin even as we are born of the husbandless earth.

It is passing strange that the earth gives not to the unbelievers the roots that would suck at her breast, nor the wings wherewith to fly high and drink and be filled with the dews of her space.

But I know what I know, and it is enough.

LOVE'S WILD ASSAULT

[The ancient Earth Gods conclude that their weariness with life is unwarranted, and that the presence of love has changed everything.]

First God:

Eternal altar!
Wouldst thou indeed this night
a god for sacrifice?
Now then I come,
and coming, I offer up
my passion and my pain.

Lo, there is the dancer,
carved out of our ancient eagerness,
and the singer is crying
mine own songs unto the wind.

And in that dancing and in that singing
a god is slain within me.
My god-heart within my human ribs
shouts to my god-heart in mid-air.

The human pit that wearied me
calls to divinity.
The beauty that we have
sought from the beginning
calls unto divinity.

I heed,
and I have measured the call,
and now I yield.

Beauty is a path
that leads to self,
self-slain.

Beat your strings!
I will walk the path.
It stretches ever to another dawn.

Third God:

Love triumphs!
The white and green of love beside a lake.
And the proud majesty of love
    in tower or balcony.
Love in a garden or in the desert untrodden—
love is our lord and master.

It is not a wanton decay of the flesh,
nor the crumbling of desire
when desire and self are wrestling.
Nor is it flesh that takes arms against the spirit.

Love rebels not.
It only leaves the trodden way
of ancient destinies
for the sacred grove,
to sing and dance
its secret to eternity.

Love is youth with chains broken,
manhood made free from the sod,
and womanhood warmed by the flame
and shining with the light of heaven
deeper than our heaven.

Love is a distant laughter in the spirit.
It is a wild assault that
hushes you to your awakening.

It is a new dawn unto the earth,
a day not yet achieved
in your eyes or mine,
but already achieved in
its own greater heart.

Brothers, my brothers!
The bride comes from the heart of dawn
and the bridegroom from the sunset.
There is a wedding in the valley—
a day too vast for recording.

Now I will rise and strip me of time and space,
and I will dance in that field untrodden,
and the dancer's feet will move with my feet.
And I will sing in that higher air,
and a human voice will throb within my voice.

We gods shall pass into the twilight,
perchance to wake to the
dawn of another world.
But love shall stay,
and its finger-marks
shall not be erased.

The blessed forge burns,
the sparks rise,
and each spark is a sun.

Better it is for us, and wiser,
to seek a shadowed nook
and sleep in our earth divinity.

And let love, human and frail,
command the coming day.

My Soul Is My Friend

A poet's voice speaks:

My soul is my friend, who consoles me in the misery and distress of life. Those who do not befriend their soul are enemies of humanity, and those who do not find human guidance within themselves will perish desperately.

Life emerges from within, and derives not from environs.

I came to say a word, and I shall say it now. But if death prevents its uttering, it will be said by tomorrow, for tomorrow never leaves a secret in the book of eternity.

I came to live in the glory of love and the light of beauty, which are the reflections of God. I am here living, and the people are unable to exile me from the domain of life, for they know I will live in death.

If they pluck out my eyes, I will hearken to the murmurs of love and the songs of beauty.

If they close my ears, I will enjoy the touch of the breeze mixed with the incense of love and the fragrance of beauty.

If they place me in a vacuum, I will live together with my soul, the child of love and beauty.

I came here to be for all and with all, and what I do today in my solitude will be echoed by tomorrow to the people.

What I say now with one heart will be said tomorrow by many hearts.

Staying and Going

My house says to me,
"Do not leave me, for here dwells your past."

And the road says to me,
"Come and follow me, for I am your future."

And I say to both my house and the road,
"I have no past, nor have I a future.
If I stay here, there is a going in my staying.
And if I go, there is a staying in my going.
Only love and death will change all things."

My Longing Shall Gather

A little while,
and my longing shall gather
dust and foam
for another body.

A little while,
a moment of rest upon the wind,
and another woman shall bear me.

Farewell to you and
the youth I have spent with you.

It was but yesterday
we met in a dream.

You have sung to me
in my aloneness,
and I of your longings
have built a tower in the sky.

Sources of the Selections

Spirits Rebellious (1908) SR
The Broken Wings (1912) BW
A Tear and A Smile (1914) TS
The Procession (1918) TP
The Madman (1918) M
The Forerunner (1920) F
The Prophet (1923) P
Sand and Foam (1926) SF
Jesus The Son of Man (1928) JSM
The Earth Gods (1931) EG
The Wanderer (1932) W
The Garden of the Prophet (1933) GP
Lazarus and His Beloved (1933) LB

Love's Initiation

The Spring of Love (TS) from "The Life of Love"
Beauty in the Heart (SF)
First Love (BW)
Wandering Desire (F)
Singing the Heart (SF)
Beauty and Love (BW)
If You Have Desires . . . (P)
Describing First Love (BW)
Mistaken Identity (W)
Love's Summer (TS) from "The Life of Love"
O Love (F)
Desire Is Half (SF)
Between Desire and Peace (SF)
God Moves in Passion (P)
Voices in Rapture (EG)
Your Body Is the Harp of Your Soul (P)
If Your Heart Is a Volcano (SF)
Love Across Age (W)
A Desire Unfulfilled (JSM)
A Passion Unspent (W)
All the Stars of My Night Faded Away (JSM)

The Veils of Love

Love's Gifts (BW)
The Caged Heart (TS) "Vision"
Love v. Law (SR) "Madam Rose Hanie"
Three Persons Separated (BW)
What Lovers Embrace (SF)
Two Kinds of Love (W)
Whom Do We Love? (SF)
Laughter and Tears (TS)
Love Cleansed by Tears (BW)
A Woman's Heart (BW)
Love Caresses and Threshes (P)
Love's Autumn (TS) from "The Life of Love"
Between Heart and Soul (TS) from "The Victors"
Tears and Dewdrops (SF)
Depth (P)
Where Are You Now, My Other Self? (TS)
Who Is Crucifying the Sun? (JSM)
Seasons of Your Heart (P)
Great Longing (M)
Longing Beyond Words (SF)
Alone? (GP)
Unsealing the Heart (SF)

Speaking and Listening to the Heart (SF)
Freedom and Slavery (SF)
Weep for the Beloved. . . . (SM)
Harvesting the Heart's Pain (TS) from "A Poet's Voice."

ALL OUR RELATIONSHIPS

Mother (BW)
The Song that Lies Silent (SF)
Sayings on Children (SF)
Lullabies (SF)
If Love Were in the Flesh . . . (JSM)
Hide and Seek (SF)
Love Song (W)
Love and Hate (W)
Two Sides (M)
The Hermit, the Beasts and Love (W)
Working with Love (P)
Wave a Bit Nearer. . . . (W)
Sayings on Enemies (SF)
Friends and Strangers (JSM)
Friendship—Hours to Live (P)
Friendship's Sweet Responsibility (SF)

Loving the Neighbor (SF)
Your Neighbor Is Your Unknown Self (JSM)
The Neighbor Unbefriended (GP)
Your Neighbor Is a Field (JSM)
Love and Patriotism (TS) from "A Poet's Voice."
Spaces in Your Togetherness (P)
Flame to Flame (EG)
Loving the Lost Sheep (JSM)
The Fingers of One Loving Hand (TS) from "A Poet's Voice."

A LOVE BEYOND

Love's Winter (TS) from "The Life of Love"
A Rhythm for Lovers (GP)
Love Is the Only Freedom (BW)
Love Is Justice (TS) from "A Poet's Voice."
Silence Whispers to the Heart (BW)
Love Song of the Wave (TS)
Seeds of Heart (SF)
Song of Love (TS)
Love's Light (SF)
Love Is Sufficient to Itself (P)
When Love Becomes Vast (JSM) "John of Patmos"

Out of My Deeper Heart (F)

Longing for the Heart of the Beloved (LB)

Love and Time (P)

Love Created in a Moment (BW)

The Gardens of our Passion (JSM)

Love's Wild Assault (EG)

My Soul Is My Friend (TS) from "A Poet's Voice."

Staying and Going (SF)

My Longing Shall Gather (P)

About the Author

Dates from the life of Gibran Khalil Gibran, the author's full Arabic name, which due to a registration spelling mistake at his first school in the United States was changed from the usual spelling to "Kahlil."

1883:   Born in Bsharri, a village in the north of Lebanon.

1895:   Gibran's mother immigrates to Boston with her four children, hoping to flee poverty and unhappiness, while her husband remains in Lebanon, imprisoned for embezzling from the government.

1898: Returns to Lebanon to study Arabic and French at a Maronite-run pre-paratory school in Beirut. By some accounts, his mother wants to remove him from unsavory artistic influences in Boston.

1902: Returns to Boston. In fifteen months' time, he loses his mother, sister, and half-brother to tuberculosis.

1904: Through photographer Fred Holland Day he meets Mary Haskell, a school headmistress who becomes his patron, muse, editor, and possible lover. Publishes several poems in prose gathered later under the title *A Tear and a Smile*.

1908-10: Funded by Mary, he attends art school in Paris.

1911: Settles in New York where he starts an intimate correspondence with May Ziadeh, a Lebanese intellectual living in Cairo.

1918:   *The Madman*, Gibran's first book writ-
          ten in English, is published.

1920:   Together with other Arab and
          Lebanese writers and poets living
          in the United States, he founds a
          literary society called *Al Rabita al
          Qalamiyyah* (The Pen Bond).

1923:   *The Prophet* is published, with imme-
          diate success. He begins a friend-
          ship with Barbara Young, who later
          becomes his new muse and editor.

1928:   *Jesus The Son of Man* is published.

1931:   Dies in a hospital in New York at the
          age of 48, due to cirrhosis of the liver.
          As was his wish, Gibran's body is
          transferred in 1932 to Lebanon and is
          buried in his native town of Bsharri.
          An old monastery is purchased, which
          becomes a museum to his memory.

These bare facts belie the complexity and
turbulence of Kahlil Gibran's life, both inner and

outer. As one of his biographers, Suheil Bushrui, writes:

> The more that has been written about Gibran, the more elusive the man himself has tended to become, as critics, friends, and biographers have built up a variety of unconnected pictures. Gibran himself is partly to blame. He wrote very little about his own life and in recurrent moments of insecurity and "vagueness," particularly during his first years of recognition, often fabricated or embellished his humble origins and troubled background. This self-perpetuation of his myth—a tendency followed by other literary figures such as Yeats and Swift—was not intellectual dishonesty, but a manifestation of the poetic mind's desire to create its own mythology. (Bushrui, 1998).

A good online biography can be found at the website of the Gibran National Committee: *www.gibrankhalilgibran.org*.

As Bushrui notes, the many biographies and biographical studies of Gibran do not agree on many points. They are very much like the different voices presented in Gibran's book *Jesus The Son of Man*, each reporting various facets of a person who embraced both the highs and lows, the lights and shadows of a fully human life.

A selection of the biographies and collections of Gibran's letters is below.

Bushrui, S., and J. Jenkins. (1998). *Kahlil Gibran: Man and Poet*. Oxford: Oneworld.

Bushrui, S., and S. H. al-Kuzbari (eds. and trans.), (1995). *Gibran: Love Letters*. Oxford: Oneworld.

Gibran, J. and K. Gibran. (1974). *Kahlil Gibran: His Life and World*. Boston: New York Graphic Society.

Gibran, J. and K. Gibran. (2017). *Kahlil Gibran: Beyond Borders*. (Updated version of the 1974 book). Northampton, MA: Interlink Books.

Hilu, V. (1972). *Beloved Prophet: The Love Letters of Kahlil Gibran and Mary Haskell and Her Private Journal.* New York: Alfred Knopf.

Naimy, M. (1950). *Kahlil Gibran: A Biography.* New York: Philosophical Library.

Waterfield, R. (1998). *Prophet: The Life and Times of Kahlil Gibran.* New York: St. Martin's Press.

Young, B. (1945). *This Man from Lebanon: A Study of Kahlil Gibran.* New York: Alfred Knopf.

About the Editor

Photo by William A. Matheiu

Neil Douglas-Klotz, PhD is a renowned writer in the fields of Middle Eastern spirituality and the translation and interpretation of the ancient Semitic languages of Hebrew, Aramaic, and Arabic. Living in Scotland, he directs the Edinburgh Institute for Advanced Learning and for many years was cochair of the Mysticism Group of the American Academy of Religion.

A frequent speaker and workshop leader, he is the author of several books. His books on the Aramaic spirituality of Jesus include *Prayers of the Cosmos, The Hidden Gospel, Original Meditation: The Aramaic Jesus and the Spirituality of Creation,* and *Blessings of the Cosmos.* His books on a comparative view of "native" Middle Eastern spirituality include *Desert Wisdom: A Nomad's Guide to Life's Big Questions* and *The Tent of Abraham* (with Rabbi Arthur Waskow and Sr. Joan Chittister). His books on Sufi spirituality include *The Sufi Book of Life: 99 Pathways of the Heart for the Modern Dervish* and *A Little Book of Sufi Stories.* His biographical collections of the works of his Sufi teachers include *Sufi Vision and Initiation* (Samuel L. Lewis) and *Illuminating the Shadow* (Moineddin Jablonski). He has also written a mystery novel set in the first century C.E. Holy Land entitled *A Murder at Armageddon.*

For more information about his work, see the website of the Abwoon Network *www.abwoon .org* or his Facebook page *https://www.facebook .com/AuthorNeilDouglasKlotz/.*

Hampton Roads
Publishing Company

. . . for the evolving human spirit

Hampton Roads Publishing Company publishes books on a variety of subjects, including spirituality, health, and other related topics.

For a copy of our latest trade catalog, call (978) 465-0504 or visit our distributor's website at *www.redwheelweiser.com*. You can also sign up for our newsletter and special offers by going to *www.redwheelweiser.com/newsletter/*.